THIS PLANNER BELOI

ROBERTS

CLIENT TRACKING BOOK

A

Customer#.	Customer Name .

Address.

Phone No.	Email.

Occupation.	Birthday.

Appointment Day	Time.	Service	Amount	Remarks.

CLIENT TRACKING BOOK

A

Customer#.		Customer Name .		
Address.				
Phone No.		Email.		
Occupation.		Birthday.		

Appointment Day	Time.	Service	Amount	Remarks.

CLIENT TRACKING BOOK

A

Customer#.		Customer Name .			
Address.					
Phone No.		Email.			
Occupation.		Birthday.			

Appointment Day	Time.	Service	Amount	Remarks.

CLIENT TRACKING BOOK

A

Customer#.		Customer Name .			
Address.					
Phone No.		Email.			
Occupation.		Birthday.			

Appointment Day	Time.	Service	Amount	Remarks.

CLIENT TRACKING BOOK

B

Customer#.		Customer Name .		
Address.				
Phone No.		Email.		
Occupation.		Birthday.		

Appointment Day	Time.	Service	Amount	Remarks.

CLIENT TRACKING BOOK

B

Customer#.		Customer Name .		
Address.				
Phone No.		Email.		
Occupation.		Birthday.		

Appointment Day	Time.	Service	Amount	Remarks.

CLIENT TRACKING BOOK

Customer#.			Customer Name .		
Address.					
Phone No.			Email.		
Occupation.			Birthday.		

Appointment Day	Time.	Service	Amount	Remarks.

CLIENT TRACKING BOOK

B

Customer#.			Customer Name .		

Address.					

Phone No.			Email.		

Occupation.			Birthday.		

Appointment Day	Time.	Service	Amount	Remarks.

CLIENT TRACKING BOOK

C

Customer#.			Customer Name .		

Address.

Phone No.			Email.		

Occupation.			Birthday.		

Appointment Day	Time.	Service	Amount	Remarks.

CLIENT TRACKING BOOK

C

Customer#.		Customer Name .		
Address.				
Phone No.		Email.		
Occupation.		Birthday.		

Appointment Day	Time.	Service	Amount	Remarks.

CLIENT TRACKING BOOK

C

Customer#.			Customer Name .		
Address.					
Phone No.			Email.		
Occupation.			Birthday.		

Appointment Day	Time.	Service	Amount	Remarks.

CLIENT TRACKING BOOK

C

Customer#.		Customer Name .			
Address.					
Phone No.		Email.			
Occupation.		Birthday.			
Appointment Day	Time.	Service		Amount	Remarks.

CLIENT TRACKING BOOK

D

Customer#.		Customer Name .		
Address.				
Phone No.		Email.		
Occupation.		Birthday.		

Appointment Day	Time.	Service	Amount	Remarks.

CLIENT TRACKING BOOK

D

Customer#.	Customer Name .

Address.

Phone No.	Email.

Occupation.	Birthday.

Appointment Day	Time.	Service	Amount	Remarks.

CLIENT TRACKING BOOK

D

Customer#.		Customer Name .		
Address.				
Phone No.		Email.		
Occupation.		Birthday.		

Appointment Day	Time.	Service	Amount	Remarks.

CLIENT TRACKING BOOK

Customer#.		Customer Name .			
Address.					
Phone No.		Email.			
Occupation.		Birthday.			

Appointment Day	Time.	Service	Amount	Remarks.

CLIENT TRACKING BOOK

E

Customer#.			Customer Name .		
Address.					
Phone No.			Email.		
Occupation.			Birthday.		

Appointment Day	Time.	Service	Amount	Remarks.

CLIENT TRACKING BOOK

E

Customer#.		Customer Name .		
Address.				
Phone No.		Email.		
Occupation.		Birthday.		

Appointment Day	Time.	Service	Amount	Remarks.

CLIENT TRACKING BOOK

E

Customer#.			Customer Name .		

Address.					

Phone No.			Email.		

Occupation.			Birthday.		

Appointment Day	Time.	Service	Amount	Remarks.

CLIENT TRACKING BOOK

Customer#.		Customer Name .		
Address.				
Phone No.		Email.		
Occupation.		Birthday.		

Appointment Day	Time.	Service	Amount	Remarks.

CLIENT TRACKING BOOK

F

Customer#.		Customer Name .		
Address.				
Phone No.		Email.		
Occupation.		Birthday.		

Appointment Day	Time.	Service	Amount	Remarks.

CLIENT TRACKING BOOK

F

Customer#.		Customer Name .	
Address.			
Phone No.		Email.	
Occupation.		Birthday.	

Appointment Day	Time.	Service	Amount	Remarks.

CLIENT TRACKING BOOK

F

Customer#.		Customer Name .			
Address.					
Phone No.		Email.			
Occupation.		Birthday.			

Appointment Day	Time.	Service	Amount	Remarks.

CLIENT TRACKING BOOK

Customer#.		Customer Name .		
Address.				
Phone No.		Email.		
Occupation.		Birthday.		

Appointment Day	Time.	Service	Amount	Remarks.

CLIENT TRACKING BOOK

G

Customer#.		Customer Name .		
Address.				
Phone No.		Email.		
Occupation.		Birthday.		

Appointment Day	Time.	Service	Amount	Remarks.

CLIENT TRACKING BOOK

Customer#.		Customer Name .		
Address.				
Phone No.		Email.		
Occupation.		Birthday.		

Appointment Day	Time.	Service	Amount	Remarks.

CLIENT TRACKING BOOK

Customer#.		Customer Name .			
Address.					
Phone No.		Email.			
Occupation.		Birthday.			

Appointment Day	Time.	Service	Amount	Remarks.

CLIENT TRACKING BOOK

Customer#.		Customer Name .			
Address.					
Phone No.		Email.			
Occupation.		Birthday.			

Appointment Day	Time.	Service	Amount	Remarks.

CLIENT TRACKING BOOK

H

Customer#.		Customer Name .			
Address.					
Phone No.		Email.			
Occupation.		Birthday.			

Appointment Day	Time.	Service	Amount	Remarks.

CLIENT TRACKING BOOK

Customer#.		Customer Name .		
Address.				
Phone No.		Email.		
Occupation.		Birthday.		

Appointment Day	Time.	Service	Amount	Remarks.

CLIENT TRACKING BOOK

H

Customer#.		Customer Name .			
Address.					
Phone No.		Email.			
Occupation.		Birthday.			

Appointment Day	Time.	Service	Amount	Remarks.

CLIENT TRACKING BOOK

H

Customer#.		Customer Name .			

Address.					

Phone No.		Email.			

Occupation.		Birthday.			

Appointment Day	Time.	Service	Amount	Remarks.

CLIENT TRACKING BOOK

Customer#.	Customer Name .

Address.

Phone No.	Email.
Occupation.	Birthday.

Appointment Day	Time.	Service	Amount	Remarks.

CLIENT TRACKING BOOK

Customer#.		Customer Name .		
Address.				
Phone No.		Email.		
Occupation.		Birthday.		

Appointment Day	Time.	Service	Amount	Remarks.

CLIENT TRACKING BOOK

Customer#.	Customer Name .

Address.	

Phone No.	Email.

Occupation.	Birthday.

Appointment Day	Time.	Service	Amount	Remarks.

CLIENT TRACKING BOOK

Customer#.			Customer Name .		
Address.					
Phone No.			Email.		
Occupation.			Birthday.		
Appointment Day	Time.	Service		Amount	Remarks.

CLIENT TRACKING BOOK

J

Customer#.		Customer Name .			
Address.					
Phone No.		Email.			
Occupation.		Birthday.			

Appointment Day	Time.	Service	Amount	Remarks.

CLIENT TRACKING BOOK

J

Customer#.			Customer Name .		
Address.					
Phone No.			Email.		
Occupation.			Birthday.		

Appointment Day	Time.	Service	Amount	Remarks.

CLIENT TRACKING BOOK

J

Customer#.			Customer Name .		

Address.					

Phone No.			Email.		

Occupation.			Birthday.		

Appointment Day	Time.	Service	Amount	Remarks.

CLIENT TRACKING BOOK

J

Customer#.			Customer Name .		
Address.					
Phone No.			Email.		
Occupation.			Birthday.		

Appointment Day	Time.	Service	Amount	Remarks.

CLIENT TRACKING BOOK

K

Customer#.		Customer Name .			
Address.					
Phone No.		Email.			
Occupation.		Birthday.			

Appointment Day	Time.	Service	Amount	Remarks.

CLIENT TRACKING BOOK

K

Customer#.		Customer Name .			
Address.					
Phone No.		Email.			
Occupation.		Birthday.			

Appointment Day	Time.	Service	Amount	Remarks.

CLIENT TRACKING BOOK

K

Customer#.	Customer Name .

Address.

Phone No.	Email.

Occupation.	Birthday.

Appointment Day	Time.	Service	Amount	Remarks.

CLIENT TRACKING BOOK

K

Customer#.		Customer Name .			
Address.					
Phone No.		Email.			
Occupation.		Birthday.			

Appointment Day	Time.	Service	Amount	Remarks.

CLIENT TRACKING BOOK

L

Customer#.		Customer Name .			

Address.					

Phone No.		Email.			

Occupation.		Birthday.			

Appointment Day	Time.	Service	Amount	Remarks.

CLIENT TRACKING BOOK

Customer#.		Customer Name .		
Address.				
Phone No.		Email.		
Occupation.		Birthday.		

Appointment Day	Time.	Service	Amount	Remarks.

CLIENT TRACKING BOOK

L

Customer#.	Customer Name .

Address.

Phone No.	Email.

Occupation.	Birthday.

Appointment Day	Time.	Service	Amount	Remarks.

CLIENT TRACKING BOOK

L

Customer#.			Customer Name .		
Address.					
Phone No.			Email.		
Occupation.			Birthday.		

Appointment Day	Time.	Service	Amount	Remarks.

CLIENT TRACKING BOOK

M

Customer#.		Customer Name .			
Address.					
Phone No.		Email.			
Occupation.		Birthday.			

Appointment Day	Time.	Service	Amount	Remarks.

CLIENT TRACKING BOOK

M

Customer#.		Customer Name .		
Address.				
Phone No.		Email.		
Occupation.		Birthday.		

Appointment Day	Time.	Service	Amount	Remarks.

CLIENT TRACKING BOOK

M

Customer#.		Customer Name .			
Address.					
Phone No.		Email.			
Occupation.		Birthday.			

Appointment Day	Time.	Service	Amount	Remarks.

CLIENT TRACKING BOOK

Customer#.	Customer Name .

Address.

Phone No.	Email.

Occupation.	Birthday.

Appointment Day	Time.	Service	Amount	Remarks.

CLIENT TRACKING BOOK

N

Customer#.		Customer Name .		
Address.				
Phone No.		Email.		
Occupation.		Birthday.		

Appointment Day	Time.	Service	Amount	Remarks.

CLIENT TRACKING BOOK

Customer#.		Customer Name .		
Address.				
Phone No.		Email.		
Occupation.		Birthday.		

Appointment Day	Time.	Service	Amount	Remarks.

CLIENT TRACKING BOOK

Customer#.		Customer Name .			
Address.					
Phone No.		Email.			
Occupation.		Birthday.			

Appointment Day	Time.	Service	Amount	Remarks.

CLIENT TRACKING BOOK

Customer#.		Customer Name .		
Address.				
Phone No.		Email.		
Occupation.		Birthday.		

Appointment Day	Time.	Service	Amount	Remarks.

CLIENT TRACKING BOOK

O

Customer#.	Customer Name .

Address.

Phone No.	Email.

Occupation.	Birthday.

Appointment Day	Time.	Service	Amount	Remarks.

CLIENT TRACKING BOOK

Customer#.		Customer Name .		
Address.				
Phone No.		Email.		
Occupation.		Birthday.		

Appointment Day	Time.	Service	Amount	Remarks.

CLIENT TRACKING BOOK

O

Customer#.	Customer Name .
Address.	
Phone No.	Email.
Occupation.	Birthday.

Appointment Day	Time.	Service	Amount	Remarks.

CLIENT TRACKING BOOK

Customer#.	Customer Name .
Address.	
Phone No.	Email.
Occupation.	Birthday.

Appointment Day	Time.	Service	Amount	Remarks.

CLIENT TRACKING BOOK

P	

Customer#.	Customer Name .

Address.

Phone No.	Email.
Occupation.	Birthday.

Appointment Day	Time.	Service	Amount	Remarks.

CLIENT TRACKING BOOK

P

Customer#.			Customer Name .		
Address.					
Phone No.			Email.		
Occupation.			Birthday.		

Appointment Day	Time.	Service	Amount	Remarks.

CLIENT TRACKING BOOK

P

Customer#.		Customer Name .			
Address.					
Phone No.		Email.			
Occupation.		Birthday.			

Appointment Day	Time.	Service	Amount	Remarks.

CLIENT TRACKING BOOK

Customer#.		Customer Name .			
Address.					
Phone No.		Email.			
Occupation.		Birthday.			

Appointment Day	Time.	Service	Amount	Remarks.

CLIENT TRACKING BOOK

Q	

Customer#.	Customer Name .

Address.

Phone No.	Email.

Occupation.	Birthday.

Appointment Day	Time.	Service	Amount	Remarks.

CLIENT TRACKING BOOK

Q

Customer#.		Customer Name .		
Address.				
Phone No.		Email.		
Occupation.		Birthday.		

Appointment Day	Time.	Service	Amount	Remarks.

CLIENT TRACKING BOOK

Q

Customer#.		Customer Name .		
Address.				
Phone No.		Email.		
Occupation.		Birthday.		

Appointment Day	Time.	Service	Amount	Remarks.

CLIENT TRACKING BOOK

Q

Customer#.		Customer Name .		

Address.				

Phone No.		Email.		

Occupation.		Birthday.		

Appointment Day	Time.	Service	Amount	Remarks.

CLIENT TRACKING BOOK

R

Customer#.			Customer Name .		
Address.					
Phone No.			Email.		
Occupation.			Birthday.		

Appointment Day	Time.	Service	Amount	Remarks.

CLIENT TRACKING BOOK

R

Customer#.		Customer Name .			
Address.					
Phone No.		Email.			
Occupation.		Birthday.			

Appointment Day	Time.	Service	Amount	Remarks.

CLIENT TRACKING BOOK

R

Customer#.		Customer Name .		
Address.				
Phone No.		Email.		
Occupation.		Birthday.		

Appointment Day	Time.	Service	Amount	Remarks.

CLIENT TRACKING BOOK

R

Customer#.		Customer Name .			
Address.					
Phone No.		Email.			
Occupation.		Birthday.			

Appointment Day	Time.	Service	Amount	Remarks.

CLIENT TRACKING BOOK

S

Customer#.		Customer Name .		
Address.				
Phone No.		Email.		
Occupation.		Birthday.		

Appointment Day	Time.	Service	Amount	Remarks.

CLIENT TRACKING BOOK

S

Customer#.		Customer Name .		
Address.				
Phone No.		Email.		
Occupation.		Birthday.		

Appointment Day	Time.	Service	Amount	Remarks.

CLIENT TRACKING BOOK

S

Customer#.	Customer Name .

Address.	

Phone No.	Email.

Occupation.	Birthday.

Appointment Day	Time.	Service	Amount	Remarks.

CLIENT TRACKING BOOK

S

Customer#.			Customer Name .		
Address.					
Phone No.			Email.		
Occupation.			Birthday.		

Appointment Day	Time.	Service	Amount	Remarks.

CLIENT TRACKING BOOK

T

Customer#.		Customer Name .		
Address.				
Phone No.		Email.		
Occupation.		Birthday.		

Appointment Day	Time.	Service	Amount	Remarks.

CLIENT TRACKING BOOK

Customer#.		Customer Name .			
Address.					
Phone No.		Email.			
Occupation.		Birthday.			

Appointment Day	Time.	Service	Amount	Remarks.

CLIENT TRACKING BOOK

Customer#.		Customer Name .		

Address.				

Phone No.		Email.		

Occupation.		Birthday.		

Appointment Day	Time.	Service	Amount	Remarks.

CLIENT TRACKING BOOK

T

Customer#.		Customer Name .		
Address.				
Phone No.		Email.		
Occupation.		Birthday.		

Appointment Day	Time.	Service	Amount	Remarks.

CLIENT TRACKING BOOK

U

Customer#.		Customer Name .			
Address.					
Phone No.		Email.			
Occupation.		Birthday.			

Appointment Day	Time.	Service	Amount	Remarks.

CLIENT TRACKING BOOK

U

Customer#.		Customer Name .		

Address.

Phone No.		Email.		

Occupation.		Birthday.		

Appointment Day	Time.	Service	Amount	Remarks.

CLIENT TRACKING BOOK

U

Customer#.	Customer Name .

Address.

Phone No.	Email.

Occupation.	Birthday.

Appointment Day	Time.	Service	Amount	Remarks.

CLIENT TRACKING BOOK

U

Customer#.		Customer Name .		
Address.				
Phone No.		Email.		
Occupation.		Birthday.		

Appointment Day	Time.	Service	Amount	Remarks.

CLIENT TRACKING BOOK

V	

Customer#.	Customer Name .

Address.	

Phone No.	Email.

Occupation.	Birthday.

Appointment Day	Time.	Service	Amount	Remarks.

CLIENT TRACKING BOOK

V

Customer#.			Customer Name .		
Address.					
Phone No.			Email.		
Occupation.			Birthday.		

Appointment Day	Time.	Service	Amount	Remarks.

CLIENT TRACKING BOOK

V	

Customer#.	Customer Name .

Address.	

Phone No.	Email.

Occupation.	Birthday.

Appointment Day	Time.	Service	Amount	Remarks.

CLIENT TRACKING BOOK

V

Customer#.		Customer Name .		
Address.				
Phone No.		Email.		
Occupation.		Birthday.		

Appointment Day	Time.	Service	Amount	Remarks.

CLIENT TRACKING BOOK

W

Customer#.			Customer Name .		
Address.					
Phone No.			Email.		
Occupation.			Birthday.		

Appointment Day	Time.	Service	Amount	Remarks.

CLIENT TRACKING BOOK

W

Customer#.		Customer Name .		
Address.				
Phone No.		Email.		
Occupation.		Birthday.		

Appointment Day	Time.	Service	Amount	Remarks.

CLIENT TRACKING BOOK

W

Customer#.		Customer Name .		
Address.				
Phone No.		Email.		
Occupation.		Birthday.		

Appointment Day	Time.	Service	Amount	Remarks.

CLIENT TRACKING BOOK

W

Customer#.			Customer Name .		
Address.					
Phone No.			Email.		
Occupation.			Birthday.		

Appointment Day	Time.	Service	Amount	Remarks.

CLIENT TRACKING BOOK

X

Customer#.	Customer Name .

Address.

Phone No.	Email.

Occupation.	Birthday.

Appointment Day	Time.	Service	Amount	Remarks.

CLIENT TRACKING BOOK

X

Customer#.		Customer Name .		
Address.				
Phone No.		Email.		
Occupation.		Birthday.		

Appointment Day	Time.	Service	Amount	Remarks.

CLIENT TRACKING BOOK

X	

Customer#.	Customer Name .

Address.

Phone No.	Email.

Occupation.	Birthday.

Appointment Day	Time.	Service	Amount	Remarks.

CLIENT TRACKING BOOK

X

Customer#.		Customer Name .		
Address.				
Phone No.		Email.		
Occupation.		Birthday.		

Appointment Day	Time.	Service	Amount	Remarks.

CLIENT TRACKING BOOK

Y

Customer#.		Customer Name .			
Address.					
Phone No.		Email.			
Occupation.		Birthday.			

Appointment Day	Time.	Service	Amount	Remarks.

CLIENT TRACKING BOOK

Y

Customer#.		Customer Name .			
Address.					
Phone No.		Email.			
Occupation.		Birthday.			

Appointment Day	Time.	Service	Amount	Remarks.

CLIENT TRACKING BOOK

Y

Customer#.		Customer Name .		

Address.

Phone No.		Email.		

Occupation.		Birthday.		

Appointment Day	Time.	Service	Amount	Remarks.

CLIENT TRACKING BOOK

Y

Customer#.			Customer Name .		

Address.					

Phone No.			Email.		

Occupation.			Birthday.		

Appointment Day	Time.	Service	Amount	Remarks.

CLIENT TRACKING BOOK

Z	

Customer#.	Customer Name .

Address.	

Phone No.	Email.

Occupation.	Birthday.

Appointment Day	Time.	Service	Amount	Remarks.

CLIENT TRACKING BOOK

Z

Customer#.	Customer Name .

Address.

Phone No.	Email.

Occupation.	Birthday.

Appointment Day	Time.	Service	Amount	Remarks.

CLIENT TRACKING BOOK

Z

Customer#.		Customer Name .		
Address.				
Phone No.		Email.		
Occupation.		Birthday.		

Appointment Day	Time.	Service	Amount	Remarks.

CLIENT TRACKING BOOK

Customer#.			Customer Name .		
Address.					
Phone No.			Email.		
Occupation.			Birthday.		

Appointment Day	Time.	Service	Amount	Remarks.

Made in the USA
Columbia, SC
25 August 2022

66079754R00059